Written by Brianna Hassan-Bravo

Illustrated by SIBGHAT ULLAH

Time to be Positive

When I go to bed
early and sleep the
right amount of time
that my body needs...

2

I wake up HAPPY, with a smile, positive and excited for a new day ahead.
I teach my friends to choose positive thoughts and my family and I put colorful GRATITUDE notes inside our gratitude jar.

3

I jump and move my body, appreciating the sunshine and fresh air.
I use my manners because it makes other people feel happy too!

If I can't do something the first time, I keep trying, because the more I practice, the better I become at it.
If you want to be really good at anything, you just need to practice and practice and practice...

I like the way I am. We are all special in our own unique way. I love all the things my body can do. I can choose to have the mindset to feel strong and confident. Even if I am a little person, I can still be a fast runner because the size of my body has nothing to do with it, it is the size of my MINDSET that matters the most.

I love myself just the way I am and I enjoy exploring new things to do. I can make decisions and speak up for myself. The grown-ups in my life love me too and they often remind me.

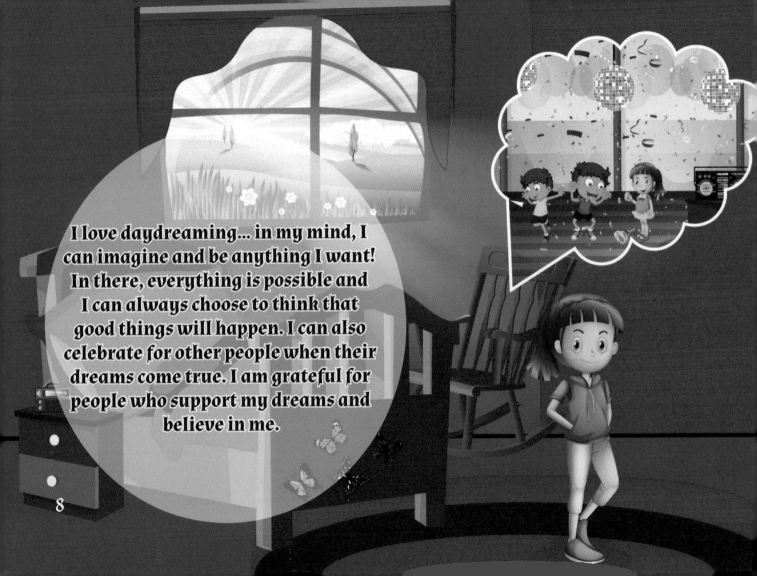

I love daydreaming... in my mind, I can imagine and be anything I want! In there, everything is possible and I can always choose to think that good things will happen. I can also celebrate for other people when their dreams come true. I am grateful for people who support my dreams and believe in me.

8

When something goes wrong or annoys me, I can choose to let it go. I know the Universe will have something bigger and better for me.

I am good at saying "I am sorry" if I hurt or offend someone else. If I spend too much time being upset, I will miss out on the other good things happening around me. I like being kind and letting mistakes go so I can be the best ME.

When something is difficult, I feel proud of myself for choosing to keep going.
I feel strong when I make decisions for myself.

11

I like to help others. Praising is a very good way to help others with their self-esteem, because they MATTER just as much as you do.

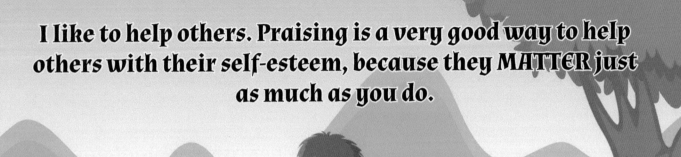

Being friendly is always a nice thing to do.

13

Eating healthy food and drinking lots of water keeps me in a good mood and full of energy. I can think positive and feel good.

ABCDEFGHIJKLMNOPQRSTUVWXYZ

I can use my creativity to come up with solutions to solve problems and share my thoughts or ask an adult for help.

HELP

I like meditating. It is important for me to spend quality quiet time on my own, enjoying the sound of the beautiful nature that surrounds me. It helps me feel peaceful, relaxed and strong.

Here is a great idea of something that makes me feel good about myself.

With the help of a grown-up, write your favorite positive statements or affirmations on thick colorful paper and stick them on your wall.

You will see how much fun it is to go to bed seeing all of those positive phrases and also waking up to them.

You can also include fun pictures of you and
your loved ones.

18

Before you go to bed, use a Success Journal to write down 5 great things you accomplished that day and be grateful for them!

I love celebrating every day whenever I do something good, or say something nice, or share with someone else, I dance to celebrate because everything is a win if you choose to see it that way.

20

On the weekend, I encourage you to make a list of all the things that you are good at. You will be excited to see how big the list it. You can ask any grown-ups around you for help.

I also encourage you to look in the mirror and talk to every part of your body, saying beautiful, loving things of why you are grateful for that part of your body.

When I feel sad, I stand in front of the mirror and smile for 1minute, I feel so much better afterwards. Try it! You will see how much fun it is.

Writing short love notes to my friends is also fun to do in the morning so I can surprise them at school.

I like having fresh flowers in my room every now and then for no reason, I deserve them and you do too.

25

I like feeling brave to try new things, it is the only
way to discover what I am good at and what I enjoy...
I love singing, dancing, acting, speaking in front of
the camera and posing for it, reading, playing piano,
playing guitar, swimming, bike riding, and playing
with my puppy Kloe.

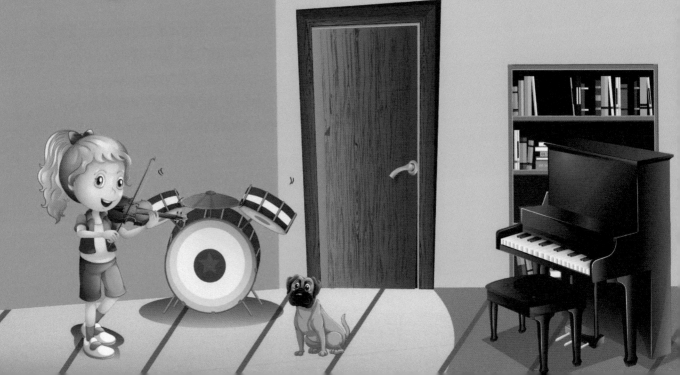

Dress in your favorite clothes that make you feel special, even if you are not going anywhere.

Make a dream board, big and colorful with all the pictures from your favorite dreams and desires, you can get a grown-up to help you find fun photos on the Internet.

28

Have you ever tried to be your own best friend? There are many rewards you can give yourself every day.

You can pat yourself on the back and say, "well done", you can smile when you think of how cool it is to be you. You can chat with a grown-up and tell them something that you're really proud of doing. And best of all, you can make a list of your goals and put a HUGE check mark next to each of them when accomplished and then celebrate!!

$$2 + 2 = 4$$
$$3 + 3 = 6$$
$$4 + 4 = 8$$

Next time you feel nervous about something, like a talk you have to do at school or meeting new friends at a party, you can rehearse and practice before hand. You can stand in front of the mirror and practice what you will do in that situation ahead of time so you can feel confident about it.

Do you laugh about your mistakes? I was at a shop with my mom the other day and as I tried to pull my top down, I accidentally pulled my skirt down in public, I could have cried in embarrassment, but instead, I chose to laugh about it and have fun with it.

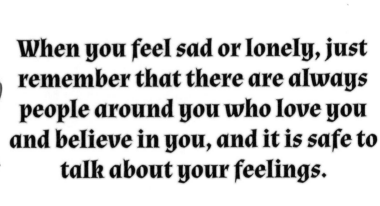

When you feel sad or lonely, just remember that there are always people around you who love you and believe in you, and it is safe to talk about your feelings.

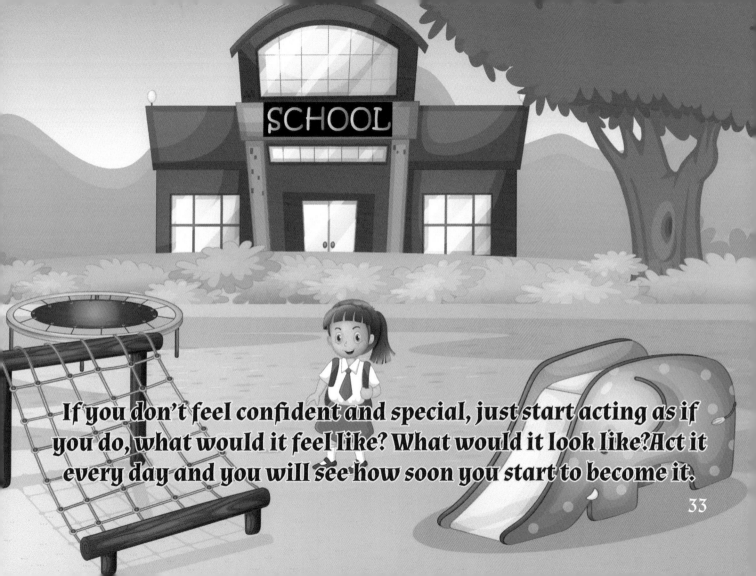

If you don't feel confident and special, just start acting as if you do, what would it feel like? What would it look like? Act it every day and you will see how soon you start to become it.

33

I hope you had fun reading my book and learning some basic tricks on how to become confident. I love doing videos for other kids on positive topics that help your self-esteem and confidence. You can watch my videos, message me, and connect with me on my Facebook fan page:

https://www.facebook.com/BreeHassanBravo/

34

Printed in Great Britain
by Amazon

13019279R00020